Nail Decorating

Nail Decorating

TIPS & TECHNIQUES FOR FABULOUS FUN

by

Rachelle Tracy

Mud Puddle
POWERING CREATIVITY

Nail Decorating:
Tips & Techniques for Fabulous Fun
by Rachelle Tracy

Photography by: Shay Design
Illustrations by: Darin Anderson
Art Director: Matt Shay
Editor: Lisa Groen
Project Manager: Brandy Shay

Mud Puddle, Inc.
36 W. 25th Street
New York, NY 10010
info@mudpuddleinc.com

ISBN: 978-1-60311-361-8

Printed in China, April 2021

11 13 15 17 18 16 14 12

Nail art is sweeping girls' fashion today. Creative nail designs serve as accessories—like jewelry—with their patterns, designs and sparkle. And the latest nail polish products and manicure kits make nail design quick and easy. With the right tools and a little practice, anyone can create fun nail art. You'll soon come up with your own unique designs. So dive in! Within no time, you, too, will express your creativity and individuality through the paint on your nails.

Contents

What You'll Need to Start

Below is a list of items you'll need to complete all of the nail art projects in this book; many may be purchased at drugstores. Specialty nail polish—like stripe polish—may be found in beauty supply stores. Art supply and craft stores stock a variety of brushes.

Base coat: helps polish adhere to the nail more easily, and provides a more even texture. Also creates a barrier for the nail to prevent staining.

Brushes: used for painting narrow lines, intricate patterns, blending and applying glitter.

Cuticle pusher: a metal or plastic tool with a curved end to push down cuticles.

Dotting tool: a metal tool with two different sized tips to make dots, petals for flowers and marbling. Also helpful for picking up and placing gemstones.

Makeup sponge: a round or wedge-shaped compressed sponge with a soft, pliable texture. Used for blending different colors of polish.

Nail polish pen: a convenient way to apply precise polish—lines, dots and other shapes.

Nail polish remover: used to remove old polish. Also helpful in tidying up cuticles and nail beds after applying polish.

Orange wood stick: a tool with two ends—beveled and pointed—for pushing down cuticles, cleaning under nails and cleaning around nail beds.

Scotch tape: serves as a guide for intricate nail designs, and comes in narrow widths to make stenciling on nails easier.

Stripe polish: a nail polish with a long, thin brush used for making precise lines, dots and other shapes.

Toothpick: used for applying polish in small lines and dots. Also used in marbling and for making flower petals.

Top coat: acts as a protective barrier to prevent nail polish from chipping and peeling. Also provides a shiny finish.

Toothpick

Small Dotting Tool

Orange Wood Stick

1" Brush

Medium Dotting Tool

¼" Brush

Large Dotting Tool

½" Brush

Design Basics

Below is a list of the basic techniques and designs found in this book. Follow these instructions to create professional-looking finishes and shapes—the most important elements to master as a nail artist! **For each of the projects that follow this section, nail polish colors are indicated, but feel free to change them as you see fit.**

Flower: Make five small dots in a circle on your nail. For one flower style leave the dots as they are. To make a variety of shaped petals you may try one of the following. To make petals, put your five small dots in a circle, let the polish dry slightly. Then drag a toothpick lightly from the center of each dot toward the outer edge of each dot. To lengthen the petal, drag the polish out more. To change the shape of the petal, drag the color in a different direction. Dot another color in the center of the flower.

Gemstone: Nail polish should be slightly wet, which will allow the gemstone to stick to the surface. Dip the tip of a dotting tool in clear polish to pick up the gemstone before placing it on the nail.

Glitter: After painting the entire nail, don't let the polish dry. Dip a small, dry paintbrush into craft glitter. Lightly brush the glitter onto the bottom half of the nail, moving toward the cuticle. Use short light strokes to pull the glitter up toward the middle of the nail, creating a fading effect.

You may also place glitter on the entire nail, in stripes, dots or shapes using a small, dry paintbrush.

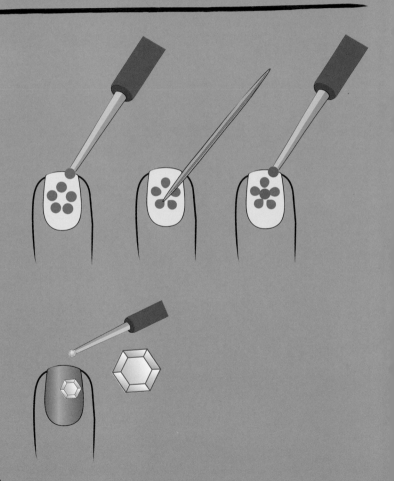

Heart: Put a small amount of polish, in a color of your choice, on a piece of scrap paper. Dip a toothpick into the polish and make two dots of color, side-by-side, on the nail. These will make the top of the heart. With the toothpick, pull the color from each dot to make the shape of the heart. You may lengthen or shorten the heart depending on how far you pull the color from the dots to the tail. Let dry completely before applying top coat.

Polka dot: Put a small amount of polish, in a color of your choice, on a piece of scrap paper. Dip the dotting tool into the polish and touch the tip of the tool to the nail. The size and number of dots on a nail is up to you!

Polka dots can be various sizes, depending on the tip of your dotting tool. To layer polka dots, make a dot and let dry. Then, make a smaller dot within the original dot, using a fine tip dotting tool and a different color polish.

Polka dots can also be used in stripe patterns. Instead of drawing solid lines, make a fine polka dot, or intersperse small dashes with dots.

9

Star: Using a dotting tool paint five evenly spaced dots in a circle on your nail. The dots will be the star's points when you're finished. Draw lines between the points to make the star. Carefully fill in the shape with polish.

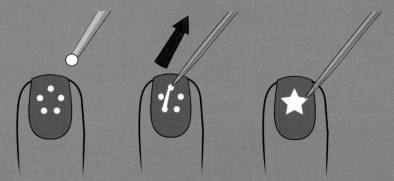

Stripe: Paint stripes over a nail that has already been painted with a color of your choice. If you have a steady hand, use a stripe polish or nail pen in a contrasting color to make the stripes. To make a more precise line, place a piece of scotch tape on the nail to serve as a guide. Draw the first straight edge of the stripe. When the polish is dry, pull off the tape and reposition for the second stripe. Reposition tape as many times as needed.

Stripes may be thick or thin, solid or dashed. Stripes may also run vertically, horizontally or diagonally.

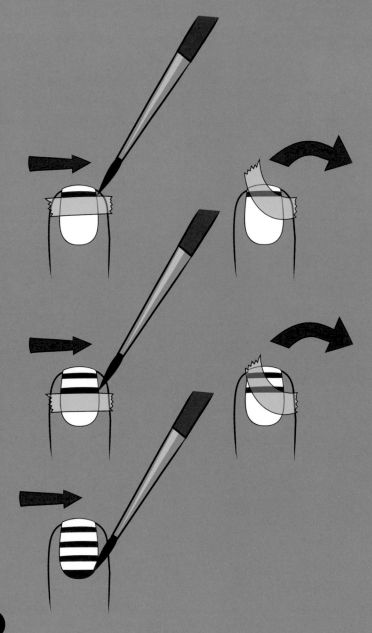

Applying Nail Polish

PROFESSIONAL TIPS

1. Before applying nail polish, push down cuticles with an orange wood stick or cuticle pusher. Always use a clear base coat to make application of polish smoother and last longer.

2. After the base coat has dried, shake selected nail color thoroughly to mix your color to the proper shade.

3. Open the nail polish and pull out the brush. Use the lip of the bottle to remove any excess polish, to prevent dripping or applying too much polish on your first coat.

4. Starting from the cuticle, place brush in the middle of the nail bed and move out to the end of the nail in one smooth stroke.

5. Using the same motion, paint the outer edges of the nail until it is completely polished.

6. Repeat these steps on each finger on both hands.

7. Apply a second coat to give nails a rich color and to make the polish last longer.

8. When finished, twist the nail polish lid tightly to avoid spills. A too-loose lid also dries out your polish.

9. Using an orange wood stick or cuticle pusher dipped in nail polish remover, go around the edge of the nail bed to remove any excess polish.

10. After polish has dried, apply a clear top coat to seal nail polish and prevent chipping and peeling. To give nails a sparkly sheen, silver or clear glitter polish may also be used as a top coat.

Musical Note

SUPPLY LIST

- **Metallic blue polish**
- **Pink polish**
- **Black stripe polish or nail pen**
- **Toothpick**
- **Dotting tool**

1. Paint nails with base coat.

2. Using metallic blue and pink polish, paint nails different colors and let dry. (Paint three nails metallic blue and two nails pink on each hand.)

3. Leave a metallic blue nail plain.

4. On a pink nail, draw a musical note. Using a dotting tool and black polish, make a diagonal teardrop at the tip of the nail. Using black stripe polish, make a line in the center of the nail, connecting it to the teardrop. At the opposite end of the line, make a horizontal line with a slight bend.

5. On a metallic blue nail, using black stripe polish or nail pen, paint diagonal stripes.

6. On a pink nail, using a dotting tool and metallic blue polish, make polka dots.

7. On a metallic blue nail, using a toothpick and pink polish, make a heart.

8. Wait for nails to dry completely and seal with a top coat.

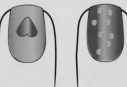

Crown

SUPPLY LIST

- Metallic white polish
- Metallic gold polish
- Metallic copper polish and stripe polish
- Toothpick
- Dotting tool
- Gemstones

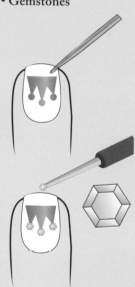

1. Paint nails with base coat.

2. Using metallic white, metallic gold and metallic copper polish, paint nails different colors and let dry. (Paint two nails metallic white and two nails metallic copper on each hand.)

3. On a metallic white nail, using a toothpick and metallic copper polish, make a heart.

4. On a metallic copper nail, using a toothpick and metallic gold polish, make a heart.

5. On the metallic gold nail, using metallic copper stripe polish, paint a stripe. Using a dotting tool, place gemstones to make another stripe.

6. On a metallic white nail, using a toothpick and metallic copper polish, draw a simple crown with three points. Fill in with color. Using a dotting tool, top points with tiny gemstones.

7. On a metallic copper nail, using a dotting tool, place one gemstone.

8. Wait for nails to dry completely and seal with a top coat.

13

Peace & Love

- Pink polish
- Yellow polish
- Orange polish
- Blue polish
- White polish
- Toothpick
- Dotting tool

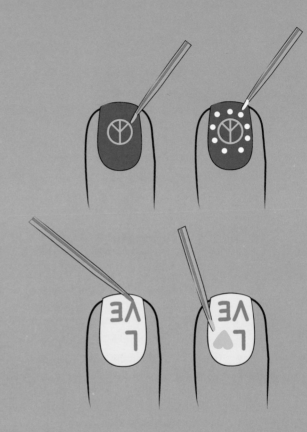

1. Paint nails with base coat.

2. Using pink, yellow, orange and blue polish, paint nails different colors and let dry. (Paint two nails pink on each hand.)

3. On a pink nail, using a dotting tool, make small blue, pink, green and white polka dots.

4. On the yellow nail, using a toothpick and orange polish, write the word LOVE, leaving an empty space for the O. Using a toothpick and blue polish, make a heart in place of the O.

5. On the orange nail, using a toothpick and green polish, make a heart.

6. On a pink nail, using a toothpick and blue polish, draw a peace sign and let dry. Then using a dotting tool or toothpick and white polish, encircle the peace sign in tiny polka dots.

7. On the blue nail, using orange stripe polish, make two narrow diagonal stripes. Using a dotting tool and orange polish, make one dotted stripe alongside the two stripes.

8. Wait for nails to dry completely and seal with a top coat.

Flower

SUPPLY LIST

- Metallic light blue polish
- Metallic pink polish
- Metallic light gold polish
- Metallic orange polish
- Gemstones
- Dotting tool

1. Paint nails with base coat.

2. Using metallic light blue, metallic pink, metallic light gold and metallic orange polish, paint nails different colors and let dry. (Paint two nails metallic pink on each hand.)

3. On both metallic pink nails, using a dotting tool and metallic light gold polish, make flower petals. Using a dotting tool, place a clear gemstone in the center of the flower.

4. On the metallic light blue nail, using a dotting tool and metallic orange polish, make flower petals. Using a dotting tool, place a pink gemstone in the center of the flower.

5. On the metallic light gold nail, using a dotting tool and metallic pink polish, make flower petals. Using a dotting tool, place a pink gemstone in the center of the flower.

6. On the metallic orange nail, using a dotting tool and metallic light blue polish, make flower petals. Using a dotting tool, place a clear gemstone in the center of the flower.

7. Wait for nails to dry completely and seal with a top coat.

French Manicure

SUPPLY LIST

- Pink polish
- White stripe polish or nail pen
- Gemstones
- Dotting tool

1. Paint nails with base coat.

2. Using pink polish, paint all nails and let dry.

3. Using white stripe polish, paint the tip of each nail and dry slightly.

4. Using a dotting tool, place gemstones in a line along the bottom of the white tip.

5. Wait for nails to dry completely and seal with a top coat.

Tiger Print

SUPPLY LIST

- Orange polish
- Lavender polish
- Black stripe polish or nail pen

1. Paint nails with base coat.

2. Using orange and lavender polish, paint nails different colors and le[t] dry. (Paint two nails orange and three nails lavender on each hand.[)]

3. Using black stripe polish or nail pen, start on one side of the nail and make horizontal checkmarks that begin at the outer edge and end in the center of the nail.

4. Repeat the same on the other side of the nail, slightly above or below the checkmarks on the opposite side.

5. Continue with this pattern until the nail is covered.

6. Wait for nails to dry completely and seal with a top coat.

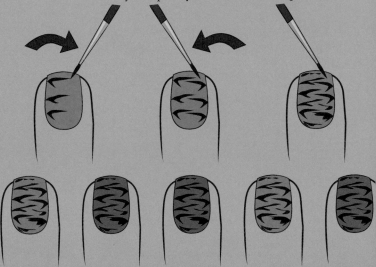

Plaid

SUPPLY LIST

- Green polish and stripe polish or nail pen
- Blue polish and stripe polish or nail pen
- Orange polish and stripe polish or nail pen
- Pink polish and stripe polish or nail pen
- Yellow polish and stripe polish or nail pen

1. Paint nails with base coat.

2. Using green, blue, orange, pink and yellow polish, paint nails different colors on each hand and let dry.

3. Using different color stripe polish, alternate painting three vertical lines, starting from the cuticle and finishing at the end of the nail, and three horizontal lines across the top half of the nail.

4. Wait for nails to dry completely and seal with a top coat.

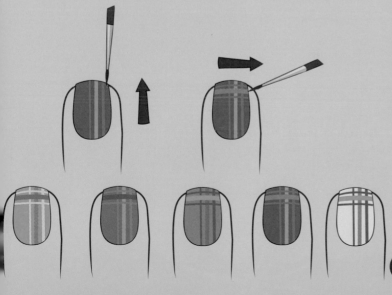

Zebra Print

SUPPLY LIST

- Pink polish
- Black stripe polish or nail pen

1. Paint nails with base coat.

2. Using pink polish, paint all of the nails and let dry.

3. Using black stripe polish or nail pen, make a slightly curved diagonal line, starting at the tip of the nail with a thick line and tapering it to a thin line that ends at the cuticle.

4. Using black stripe polish, make another slightly curved diagonal line, but begin with a thick line at the cuticle and taper it to a thin line at the tip of the nail.

5. Using black stripe polish, make small short lines, forking from the longer lines and floating in between the larger ones to finish the zebra pattern.

6. Wait for nails to dry completely and seal with a top coat.

Leopard Print

- **Pale blue polish**
- **Light pink polish**
- **Black stripe polish or nail pen**
- **Dotting tool**

1. Paint nails with base coat.

2. Using pale blue polish, paint all of the nails and let dry.

3. Using light pink polish and a dotting tool, make unsymmetrical spots on the nail. Let dry.

4. Using black stripe polish or nail pen, outline the spots. On some, outline fully. On others, outline the spots partially. The outline does not have to be precise.

5. Wait for nails to dry completely and seal with a top coat.

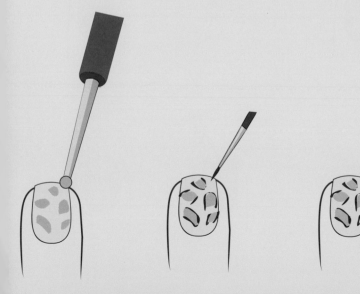

Galaxy

SUPPLY LIST

- Metallic black polish
- Metallic blue polish
- Metallic silver polish
- Metallic pink polish
- Clear, fine glitter polish
- Clear, round silver glitter polish
- Makeup sponge

1. Paint nails with base coat.

2. Using metallic black polish, paint all of the nails and let dry.

3. Using metallic blue polish, apply a small amount of color on a makeup sponge.

4. Dab the sponge onto one part of the nail until the polish feels sticky and the color is well-blended.

5. Using metallic silver polish, apply a small amount of color to the makeup sponge.

6. Dab a small dot of metallic silver on the nail, again blending well.

7. Using metallic pink polish, apply a small amount of color to the makeup sponge.

8. Dab the metallic pink over different parts of the nail, blending well.

9. Using clear, fine glitter polish, paint the nail. The nail should begin to look like a galaxy. Let dry.

10. Using clear, round silver glitter polish, dot a few pieces of the larger glitter onto each nail for stars. Don't brush the entire nail.

11. Wait for nails to dry completely and seal with a top coat.

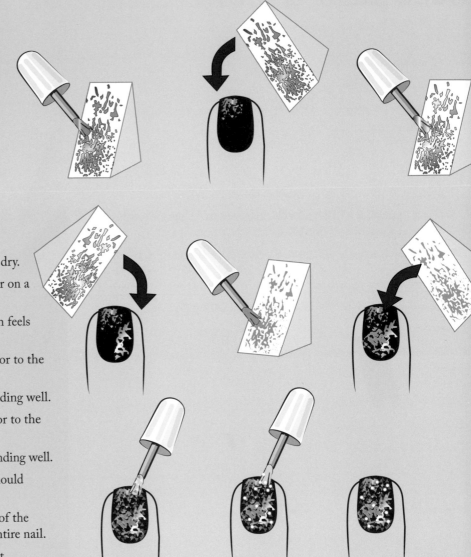

Newspaper

SUPPLY LIST

- **White polish**
- **Light pink polish**
- **Rubbing alcohol**
- **Strips of newspaper**

1. Paint nails with base coat.

2. Using white and light pink polish, paint the nails different colors and let dry. (Paint three nails white and two nails light pink on each hand.)

3. Dip one nail in a capful of rubbing alcohol. Press a strip of newspaper over the nail and hold for a few seconds. Peel off slowly. Repeat with each nail.

4. Wait for nails to dry completely and seal with a top coat.

Raised Lettering

SUPPLY LIST

- Metallic rose polish
- Metallic sage green polish
- Gemstones
- Dotting tool

1. Using metallic rose and metallic sage polish, paint the nails different colors and let dry. (Paint three nails metallic sage and two nails metallic rose on each hand.)

2. Using a dotting tool and gemstones, form letters on each nail to spell LOVE or any word you choose.

3. Wait for nails to dry completely and seal with a top coat.

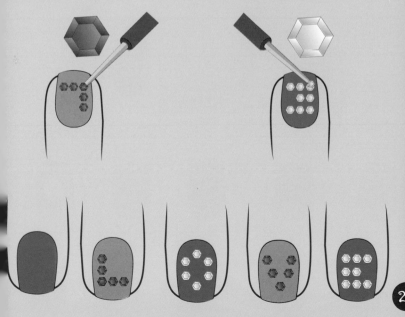

Ladybug

SUPPLY LIST

- Red polish
- Black stripe polish or nail pen
- White polish
- Toothpick
- Dotting tool

1. Paint nails with base coat.
2. Using red polish, paint all nails and let dry.
3. Leave two nails plain.
4. On one nail, using a dotting tool and black polish, make polka dots.
5. On another nail, make a lady bug. Using black stripe polish or nail pen, paint the tip of the nail.
6. Using black stripe polish or nail pen, make a vertical line in the middle of the nail, from the tip to the cuticle.
7. Using a dotting tool and black polish, make polka dots on both sides of the line.
8. Using a dotting tool and white polish, make two dots in the middle of the black tip to create eyes.
9. On the last nail, using a toothpick and white polish, make a heart.
10. Wait for nails to dry completely and seal with a top coat.

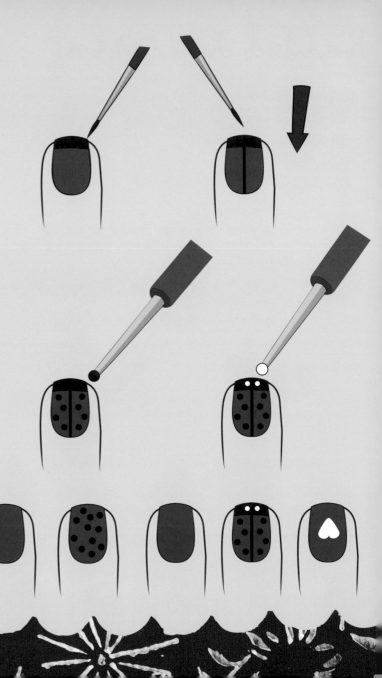

Butterfly

SUPPLY LIST

- Metallic light blue polish
- Pink glitter polish
- Gemstones
- Dotting tool
- Orange glitter polish
- Metallic yellow polish
- Toothpick

1. Paint nails with base coat.
2. Using metallic light blue polish and pink glitter polish, paint the nails different colors and let dry. (Paint three nails metallic light blue and two nails pink glitter.)
3. Leave one blue nail plain.
4. On a pink nail, using a dotting tool and metallic yellow polish, make flower petals. Place a gemstone in the center of the flower.
5. On a blue nail, draw a butterfly. Using a toothpick and orange glitter polish, make an X for the wings and let dry. Using a toothpick and metallic yellow polish, draw in the butterfly's body and head with antennae.
6. Leave one pink nail plain.
7. On the last blue nail, draw another butterfly. Using a toothpick and pink and orange glitter polish, follow the directions in step 5.
8. Wait for nails to dry completely and seal with a top coat.

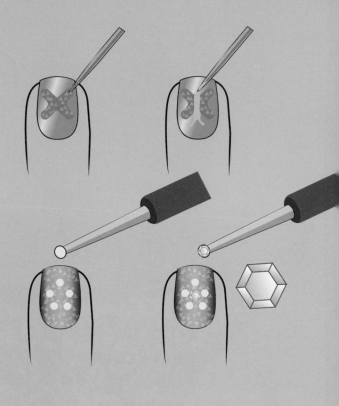

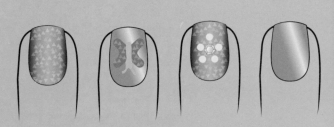

Penguin

SUPPLY LIST

- Black polish
- Purple glitter polish
- White polish
- Orange polish
- Dotting tool

1. Paint nails with base coat.
2. Using black polish, paint all the nails and let dry.
3. Using purple glitter polish, paint tip of nail and let dry.
4. Using white polish, paint lower half of nail rounding the top to create the penguin's body, and let dry.
5. Using a dotting tool and white polish, make two small dots in the center of the purple glitter polish to create eyes.
6. Using a dotting tool and orange polish, make a small triangle at the top of the white polish, to create a beak.
7. Using a dotting tool and orange polish, make two oval shapes at bottom of the white polish to create feet.
8. Using a dotting tool and black polish, make two small pupils inside the white eyes.
9. Wait for nails to dry completely and seal with a top coat.

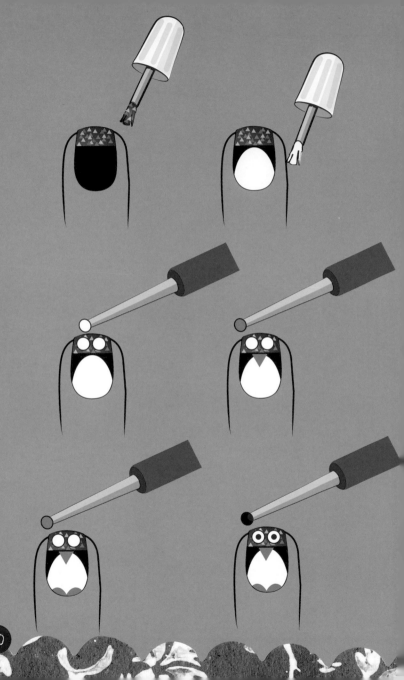

Panda

SUPPLY LIST

- Light pink polish
- White polish
- Black polish
- Dotting tool

1. Paint nails with base coat.

2. Using light pink polish, paint all of the nails and let dry.

3. Using white polish, paint a white circle for the panda's head on top half of nail and let dry.

4. Using a dotting tool and white polish, make two dots at the top of the head to create ears. Using a dotting tool and black polish, make two dots for the inside of the ears.

5. Using a dotting tool and black polish, make two dots in center of the panda's head to create eyes. Using a dotting tool and white polish, make two small pupils in the center of the eyes. Using a dotting tool and black polish, make one more dot for a nose, below the eyes.

6vv. Wait for nails to dry completely and seal with a top coat.

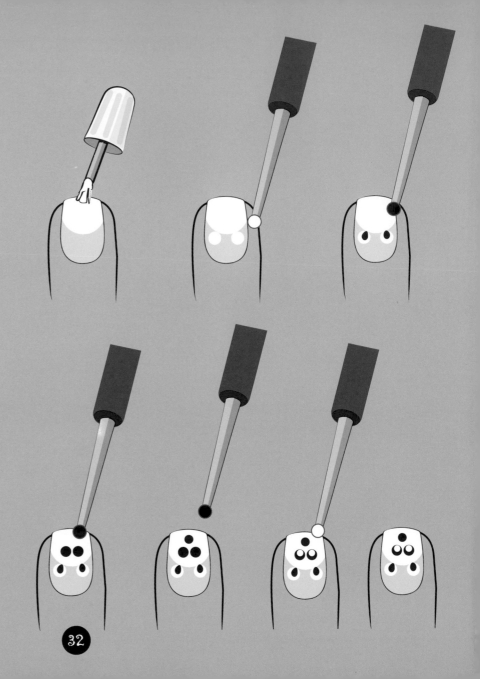

Doggie Paw Print

SUPPLY LIST

- White polish
- Black polish
- Toothpick
- Dotting tool

1. Paint nails with base coat.

2. Using white polish, paint all the nails and let dry.

3. Using a toothpick and black polish, make three upside down hearts on each nail.

4. Using a dotting tool and black polish, make three dots above each heart to create paws.

5. Wait for nails to dry completely and seal with a top coat.

Options

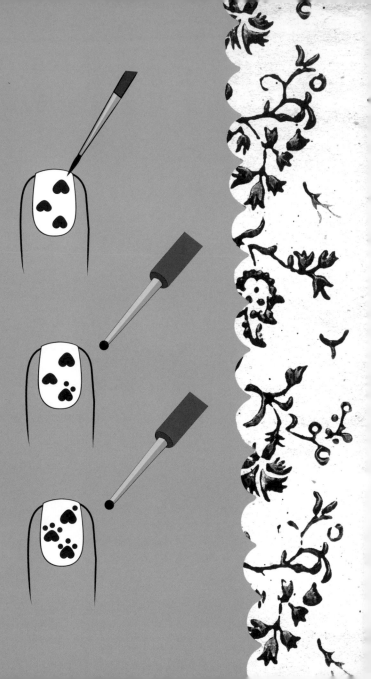

Winter Snowflakes

SUPPLY LIST

- **Metallic light blue polish**
- **White stripe polish or nail pen**
- **Clear silver glitter polish**

1. Paint nails with base coat.
2. Using metallic light blue polish, paint all the nails and let dry.
3. Using white stripe polish, create an asterisk (*) in the middle of each nail. On the end of each arm of the asterisk, draw a V to turn the symbol into a snowflake.
4. Using clear silver glitter polish, paint the entire nail and let dry.
5. Wait for nails to dry completely and seal with a top coat.

Summer Watermelon

SUPPLY LIST

- Pink polish
- Lime green stripe polish or nail pen
- Black stripe polish or nail pen
- Dotting tool

1. Paint nails with base coat.

2. Using pink polish, paint all the nails and let dry.

3. On three nails, using lime green stripe polish, paint the tip of the nail (like a French tip) and let dry. Using a black stripe polish or nail pen, create four small teardrops just below lime green line to create seeds.

4. On two nails, using a dotting tool and lime green polish, make polka dots.

5. Wait for nails to dry completely and seal with a top coat.

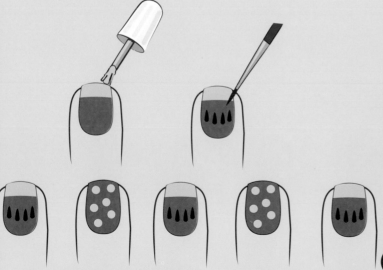

Valentine Heart for My BFF

SUPPLY LIST

- Lime green polish and stripe polish
- Pink polish
- Purple polish
- Red glitter polish
- White polish
- Toothpick
- Dotting tool

1. Paint the nails with base coat.

2. Using lime green, pink and purple polish, paint the nails different colors and let dry. (Paint two nails pink and two nails purple on each hand.)

3. Leave a purple nail plain.

4. On the lime green nail, using a toothpick and red glitter polish, make a heart in the center of the nail.

5. On a pink nail, using a toothpick and white polish, write XO.

6. On a purple nail, using a dotting tool and white polish, make polka dots.

7. On a pink nail, using lime green stripe polish, make a diagonal stripe. Using a dotting tool and lime green polish, make two dotted stripes, one on each side of the solid stripe.

8. Wait for nails to dry completely and seal with a top coat.

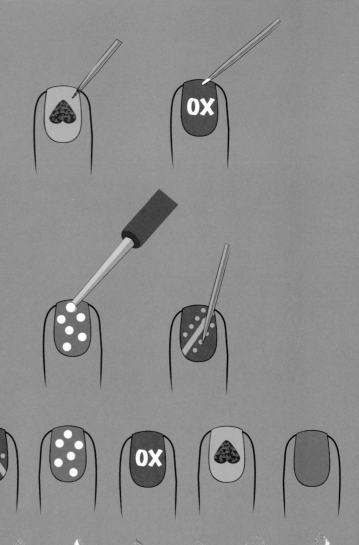

Easter Chicks

- Light blue polish
- Purple polish
- Lavender polish
- Yellow polish
- White stripe polish or nail pen
- Black stripe polish or nail pen
- Pink stripe polish or nail pen
- Orange stripe polish or nail pen
- Toothpick
- Dotting tool

1. Paint the nail with base coat.

2. Using light blue, purple, lavender and yellow polish, paint nails different colors and let dry. (Paint two nails lavender.)

3. Leave a lavender nail plain.

4. On the blue nail, using a dotting tool and purple polish, make a flower. Use pink polish for the dot in the middle of the flower.

5. On the yellow nail, make a chick. Using white stripe polish or nail pen, paint a zigzag pattern (a cracked shell) at the tip of the nail. Using black stripe polish or nail pen, make two small dots in the middle of the yellow color to create eyes. Using orange stripe polish or nail pen, make a triangle between the eyes to create a beak.

6. On the purple nail, using a dotting tool and white polish, make different sizes of polka dots.

7. On a lavender nail, using pink stripe polish or nail pen, paint diagonal stripes.

8. Wait for nails to dry completely and seal with a top coat.

Halloween Frankenstein

SUPPLY LIST

- Matte green polish
- Black stripe polish or nail pen
- White polish
- Dotting tool

1. Paint the nail with base coat.

2. Using a matte green polish, paint all the nails and let dry.

3. On three alternating nails, using black stripe polish, paint a diagonal line and fill in the top of the nail with black polish.

4. On two nails, make Frankenstein's face. Using black stripe polish or nail pen, paint an irregular line across the tip of the nail to create Frankenstein's hairline.

5. Using black stripe polish or nail pen, paint a small black stroke on either side of the nail bed to create sideburns.

6. Using a dotting tool and white polish, make two dots in the middle of green color, toward hairline, to create eyes.

7. Using black stripe polish or nail pen, make a thin short line below eyes for the mouth.

8. Using black stripe polish or nail pen, make three small black slashes through the mouth line (like stitches) to finish the mouth.

9. Using black stripe polish or nail pen, make two thin lines above the eyes, slightly curving inward to create eyebrows.

10. Using black stripe polish or nail pen, make two small dots in the center of the white eyes for pupils.

11. Wait for nails to dry completely and seal with a top coat.

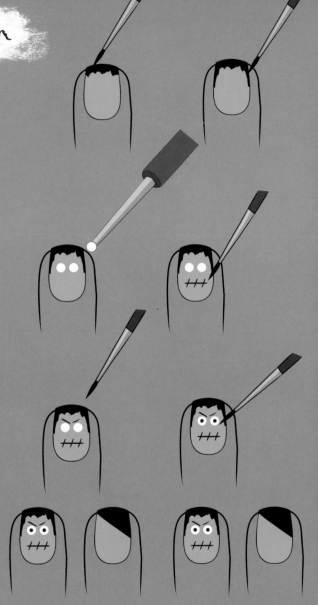

Christmas Tree

SUPPLY LIST

- Red polish
- White polish and stripe polish or nail pen
- Green polish and stripe polish or nail pen
- Silver polish
- Toothpick
- Dotting tool

1. Paint nails with base coat.

2. Using red, white, green and silver polish, paint the nails different colors and let dry. (Paint two nails red on each hand.)

3. On a red nail, using white stripe polish or nail pen, paint diagonal stripes to look like a candy cane.

4. On the white nail, using green stripe polish or nail pen, paint a simple Christmas tree.

5. On the green nail, using a dotting tool and red polish, make polka dots.

6. On the silver nail, using a toothpick and white polish, make a star.

7. On a red nail, using a toothpick and green polish, make a heart.

8. Wait for nails to dry completely and seal with a top coat.

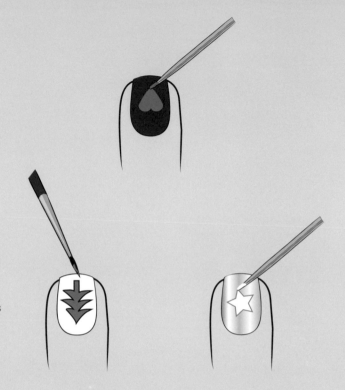

Fourth of July

SUPPLY LIST

- Red polish and stripe polish or nail pen
- White polish and stripe polish or nail pen
- Blue polish and stripe polish or nail pen
- Gemstones
- Toothpick
- Dotting tool

1. Paint nails with base coat.

2. Using red, white and blue polish, paint the nails different colors and let dry. (Paint two nails blue and two nails white on each hand.)

3. On a blue nail, using a toothpick and red polish, make a heart in the center of the nail.

4. On a white nail, using red and blue stripe polish or nail pens, make two horizontal stripes below the tip of the nail.

5. On the red nail, using a dotting tool and white polish, make a flower. Using a dotting tool, place a blue gemstone in the center of the flower.

6. On a blue nail, using white stripe polish, paint the entire nail with horizontal stripes and let dry. Using a dotting tool, place a red heart gemstone over the stripes.

7. On a white nail, using a dotting tool, place blue star gemstones in a vertical stripe in the center of the nail.

8. Wait for nails to dry completely and seal with a top coat.

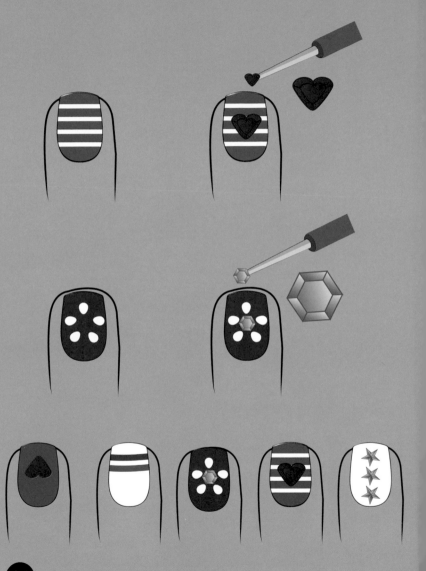